FIVE-A-

PRO

Jenny Swann and Anne Prendergast

SOUTHGATE
—PUBLISHERS—

Acknowledgements

Our thanks to the parents and pupils of Round Hill School and Arno Vale Junior School School, Nottingham, also of The Bollin School, Bowdon, Altrincham. Thanks too, to our friends and their children, who let us pick their brains relentlessly - not forgetting the lady with whom I (JS) discussed mushrooms all the way from Nottingham to London St. Pancras, to the incredulity of our fellow passengers. Peter, Bernard, Carri, Lucy, Emma, Emily and Edward - how could we have written this without you?

Thanks to the children who posed for photos: Juliette irens; Joe Parker, Nibel Akcadag and Conner Rogers. Jessie Saunders for composing the picture of 'Broccola' on page 1.
Heather Grey, Registered Nutritionist
Kenneth Isaacs (front cover photo)
Markham (Deputy Head, Pinhoe Church of England Primary School)
Jane Mackarness for valuable advice.
Linscombe Farm

Copyright © text Jenny Swann and Anne Prendergast 2006

illustrations © Creedy Images Limited 2006

First published 2006 by Southgate Publishers Ltd

Southgate Publishers Ltd, The Square, Sandford, Crediton Devon EX17 4LW

Printed and bound in Malta by Gutenberg Press Ltd

British Library Cataloguing in Publication Data

A CIP catalogue record for this book is available from the British Library

ISBN 1 85741 111 0

ISBN 9 781857 411119

Contents

- shopping
- cooking together
- snacks
- family meals
- games

Introduction

When our children were very young, and before the day when an irritating visitor told them how good they were to eat their greens, it was quite easy to shovel all sorts of fruit and veg down them. Pureed carrot, mashed banana with avocado, parsnips, puréed apple - you name it, the sweethearts tucked in.

But as they became increasingly conscious of the big, bad world out there, in which some of their friends didn't 'do' fruit or veg, and advertising encouraged them to spend all their pocket-money on junk food, the drift towards lowest-common-denominator food set in. The task of trying to make sure that our children still ate an overall balanced diet that included plenty of fruit and veg, began in earnest.

This book, which results from the ideas that we and other parents came up with in response to that challenge, helps you to avoid making some of the mistakes we made.

It's our contribution to those parents who, like us, want a few tricks up their sleeves, and recipes to hand, to persuade their children of the real pleasures of fruit and vegetables, as well as their benefits. We have tried not so much to disguise vegetables and fruit or to impose menus from on high but to interest and enthuse children. Engage their curiosity and spirit of adventure and there'll be no stopping them.

Why bother with fruit and vegetables?

There are plenty of times when one questions whether it's worth the effort, struggling against the tide of quick-fix junk food or trying to convert a child who has made up their mind not to like fruit and veg. But fruit and veg, in addition to being delicious and attractive, are important for our, and our children's, well-being.

They protect against heart disease, some forms of cancer and stroke. In addition, they are an important source of fibre, vitamins and minerals in our diet which are necessary for the health and normal functioning of our bodies. They are usually low in fat so help in weight control, too.

As well as vitamins and minerals, fruit and vegetables are rich in natural plant components known as phytochemicals. These phytochemicals give the fruit and veg their colour, flavour and smell. There are many different phytochemicals including carotenoids, phenols including flavonoids, and glucosinolates. Many are antioxidants and they play an important role in protecting the body against disease. Some vitamins are also antioxidants. Antioxidants mop up damaging chemicals in our bodies (called 'free radicals') which play role in causing cancer and other diseases. Dietary supplements such as vitamin and mineral pills do not have the same benefit as fruit and veg themselves - so it seems that they need to be taken as nature intended!

is so helpful for your children if you can establish good eating habits in childhood as
they are more likely to persist into adulthood. If your children see you enjoying fruit and
veg they will be more inclined to do so themselves. In order to heighten public awareness
of the value of a diet rich in fruit and veg and to encourage us to eat more, the five-a-day
message was launched by the government. Current recommendations are that our
children should aim for five portions a day, though the portions can be smaller than the
80g adult portion (a portion is generally a handful - growing in size as your child's hand
grows). What is less clear is how we should put this into practice. Simply eating five
portions of their favourite fruit or vegetable unfortunately doesn't count - variety is the
key to success.

The five-a-day message

We should be eating five or more portions of different fruit and vegetables each day.

- Fresh, frozen and canned fruit and veg all count.
- Potatoes do not count.
- 100% fruit juice only counts as one portion, however much is consumed, and the
  same applies to pulses.
- Nuts, seeds and jams do not count.
- Processed foods containing fruit and veg can count but you need to check the
  label, as some are high in salt and sugar.

Log onto www.5aday.nhs.uk for more information. There is also a 5-a-day chart that you
can download for your children to fill in.

Role of the common vitamins and minerals found in fruit and vegetables.

Vitamins are essential for normal growth and functioning of the body.

- Vitamin A is important for growth, healthy skin and immunity. It is an antioxidant.
- The B vitamins are made up of B1 (thiamine), B2 (riboflavin), B3 (niacin),
  B5 (panthothenic acid), B6 (pyridoxine), B7 (biotin), B9 (folic acid) and B12
  (cyanocobalamin). These vitamins work together to aid metabolism, help
  immunity, promote cell development including red blood cells and maintain a
  healthy nervous system.
- Vitamin C is an antioxidant and aids iron absorption. It is necessary for growth
  and immunity.
- Vitamin E is an antioxidant and important for the immune system.
- Vitamin K is important for bone health and blood clotting.

Minerals are another essential component of a healthy diet.

- Calcium is necessary for healthy bones and teeth.
- Magnesium is important for healthy bones and nerve and muscle function. It also controls potassium and sodium levels in the body.
- Phosphorus is needed for healthy bones and energy metabolism.
- Potassium is important for healthy cell membranes, fluid balance in the body and nerve and muscle conduction.
- Iron is important for healthy blood cells; deficiency causes anaemia. Vitamin C aids the absorption of iron.
- Manganese, zinc and copper are needed for enzyme function.
- Cromium helps insulin to work.
- Selenium is an antioxidant.

Though this list seems daunting, a diet that is varied and balanced in all food groups, not just fruit and vegetables, should provide all the body needs.

Organic is best?

There is confusion and disagreement about the benefits of organic, over non-organic, fruit and veg. As the saying goes, 'the jury is still out'. We ourselves prefer to buy organic fruit and veg when possible and affordable, but buy non-organic otherwise. And we always buy local fruit and veg if available.

Some Popular Fruit and Veg

Apples

Apples were thought to be symbols of love and beauty in Greek and Roman mythology. It is believed that the Romans brought apple cultivation to this country in the first century BC.

Apples contain flavonoids, an antioxidant, and also provide vitamin C and fibre.

Apricots

In Latin, apricot means 'precious', so called, we presume, because it ripens earlier than other summer fruits. A relative of the peach, John Ruskin described the apricot as "shining in a sweet brightness of golden velvet". It is said that Henry VIII's gardener brought the apricot to England from Italy in 1542.

The coloured flesh of apricots contains carotenoids which are converted to vitamin A and they also provide vitamin C and fibre.

Asparagus

Asparagus is a member of the lily family and grows throughout central and southern Europe, North Africa and west and central Asia. The British asparagus season is short, with asparagus being available during the early summer from late April to early July.

Asparagus contains more folic acid than most other vegetables as well as providing vitamins C, A and K. It is also a good source of fibre, potassium and other minerals.

Aubergine

It is thought that aubergines (or eggplants) were introduced to the Western world relatively recently, when they were used as decorative garden plants.

Aubergine contains antioxidant phytochemicals and is a good source of fibre and minerals such as potassium.

Avocado Pear

Avocados have been found in archaeological deposits in Mexico dating back to 7000BC. The avocado grows on evergreen trees native to the subtropics of America.

Avocados have a high energy content as they are high in monounsaturated fats. They are a good source of vitamin E, vitamin B6 and fibre.

Bananas

The word banana is derived from the Arabic meaning 'finger'. Banana plants are from the same families as lilies, orchids and palms. It is thought that if you were to lay all the bananas grown in one year end-to-end they would go round the world 2,000 times.

Bananas are high in natural sugar and a rich source of potassium. They also provide vitamin B6 and vitamin C, as well as fibre and some magnesium.

Beetroot

Wild sea beet is the ancestor of all cultivated beets. It grows in coastal areas in Europe, North Africa and Asia. The red beetroot pigment, a betaline, has been used as a dye since the 16th century and is still used today as a natural food colouring.

Beetroot contains phytochemicals which give the vegetable its colour and are antioxidant. It is an excellent source of folate and also provides fibre and minerals such as potassium.

Berries

See individual berry fruits under separate headings.

Berries are an excellent source of vitamin C and contain powerful antioxidants. These antioxidants are responsible for the colour of the skin of the berries. Blackcurrants in particular have a high vitamin C content.

Blackberries

Free and plentiful in early autumn - which child can resist blackberry picking on a warm autumn afternoon? There is evidence that blackberries were eaten in Neolithic times and many superstitions surround these fruits. In the south west of England it was believed that the first blackberry seen growing each year would get rid of warts!

The long arching prickly stems of the bramble were once known as lawyers because it was difficult to escape from them once in their clutches....

Blackberries contain vitamins C and E, fibre, folate and anthocyanins, which are the phytochemicals which give the berries their colour. They are potent antioxidants.

Blackcurrants
These can be rather fiddly to pick but seem to be plentiful at pick-your-own outlets. They last a wee bit longer if you leave the stems on when picked.

Blackcurrants are rich in vitamin C and also contain vitamin E and fibre. They contain anthocyanins which are antioxidant. These chemicals give the currants their colour and are also anti-inflammatory.

Blueberries
Blueberries are native to the United States and a close relative of the European bilberry. They contain anthocyanins, vitamin C and vitamin E. They are thought to improve memory!

Broccoli
Broccoli is a member of the brassica family of vegetables which also includes cabbage, cauliflower and Brussels sprouts. These vegetables contain chemicals which are thought to act as anti-cancer agents. The word broccoli comes from the Latin brachium meaning arm or branch.

Broccoli provides vitamin C, vitamin A, folate and fibre. It is a good source of minerals such as potassium, phosphorus and magnesium.

Butternut Squash- see Squashes

Cabbage / Greens
The Egyptians were the first people to write - with reverence! - about cabbages. The Greeks, too, held them in high esteem. Pythagoras praised them and medieval monasteries cultivated them with enthusiasm. Nowadays, they are a firm part of British life and cuisine. There are many varieties, and we consume a vast quantity of them every year.

Cabbage provides vitamins C, A and K and is a good source of folate and fibre. Dark green leafy vegetables such as greens are also a good source of iron, calcium and vitamins C, A and K. As members of the brassica family they are thought to contain potent anti-cancer agents.

Cabbages can be red, white, green or multicoloured and come in different shapes and sizes. There is no need for cabbage to be boring!

Carrots
Peter Rabbit is a good advocate for carrots if you have young children. Explain how he couldn't get enough of them! (See page 34 for games to encourage carrot consumption.)

Carrots are rich in beta-carotene which is converted into vitamin A. Carrots are also a good source of fibre and potassium.

Cauliflower
Cauliflower is made up of a compact head of underdeveloped white flower buds. The heavy green leaves that surround the head protect the flower buds from the sunlight and the head remains white.

Cauliflower, like broccoli and cabbage, is a brassica vegetable and contains glucosinolates which are thought to help fight cancer. It also provides vitamin C, folate, fibre and protein. It is a good source of the B vitamins and minerals such as potassium, magnesium, phosphorus and zinc.

Celery

In ancient Greece winning athletes were presented with bunches of celery - their equivalent of flowers today! Originally celery was used for medicinal purposes such as lowering blood pressure and it is thought to promote a good night's sleep.

Its high water content makes it a refreshing snack in summer with the added benefit of providing potassium and some vitamin C, fibre and folate.

Cherries

Cherries are thought to have been introduced to Britain by the Romans in the first century AD. Cherry stones were allegedly once used in bed warming pans!

Cherries contain anthocyanins and some potassium and vitamin C.

Corn on the Cob / Sweetcorn

Sweetcorn, or corn on the cob, is a variety of maize. It was first cultivated in America and has been an important food stuff for thousands of years. It is now cultivated in Europe, including the south of England.

Corn on the cob is not strictly a vegetable but a cereal, although it does still count towards your five-a-day. It is a starchy food and provides dietary fibre, protein and magnesium as well as some vitamin C, A and B.

Cucumber

Cucumbers are one of the oldest cultivated vegetables and are thought to have originated in India. Cucumbers belong to the squash family. Cucumber is mainly made up of water but has some vitamin C, minerals and fibre. The high water content makes it very refreshing in summer.

Gooseberries

Gooseberries have been grown in Britain for centuries. Many years ago, the juice of gooseberries was used as a treatment for fevers. They contain vitamin C, fibre and carotenoids.

Grapes

Grapes have grown wild since prehistoric times. They are rich in flavonoids which are excellent for health. It is these flavonoids which provide the antioxidant properties of wine - now believed to be good for your heart, in moderation. Adults only! Grapes also provide some vitamin C and potassium.

Green / French Beans

What makes French beans French? In fact, most green beans on our supermarket shelves come from Africa. The European season for French beans is from June to October. Green beans provide vitamins C, A and K. They are also a good source of folate, fibre and many minerals such as potassium and calcium.

Kiwis

Kiwis are originally from China and are known as Chinese gooseberries. The New Zealanders saw the market for exportation and called them kiwis. Although they are sometimes eaten skin and all in New Zealand, here we don't eat the skin.

Kiwis are a good source of vitamin C and also provide fibre, some vitamin A and minerals. They are rich in phytochemicals.

Lemons

Lemons were given to sailors in the British Navy in the 1800s to combat scurvy on long voyages. Hence the British were known as 'limeys' though now it is thought that the fruit given was indeed lemons, not limes. Citrus fruits in general are an excellent source of vitamin C, especially the peel, and also contain flavonoids.

Mangetout

Mangetout is French for 'eat all' and that is exactly what you do. A lot of children who are picky about green vegetables nonetheless like mangetout as it has quite a sweet taste. Mangetout contains vitamins C, A and B vitamins as well as folate, fibre and minerals such as potassium and calcium.

Mangoes

The wild mango originated in the foothills of the Himalayas of India and Burma. Today, India's main fruit crop is still the mango. It is held in high esteem by Hindus as old Sanskrit writings reveal a legend of deep love and beauty that sprang from the mango tree.

The coloured flesh of mangoes contains carotene which is converted to vitamin A. They are a good source of fibre and vitamin C and also provide some vitamin E. Mangoes contain a tenderizing enzyme thought to aid digestion.

Melon

There are several varieties of melon, each with a slightly different taste. Try galia or cantaloupe for a positive response from your children. To tell if a melon is ripe, press the base, which should have a little give in it. Also, the melon should be giving off a slight smell. The coloured flesh varieties such as cantaloupe melons contain carotene which is converted to vitamin A. In addition melons provide vitamin C.

Mushrooms

Mushrooms are not vegetables at all but fungi. They can be cultivated but are also found growing wild. Organisations such as the National Trust sometimes run 'foraging for fungi' days which may enthuse your children. Never pick mushrooms yourself without an expert present!

Mushrooms are high in minerals such as potassium, phosphorus, copper and selenium (an antioxidant) as well as containing vitamins such as the B vitamins and some folate.

Olives

The Greeks considered olives to be a symbol of goodness and nobility. Even today the branches of the olive tree are a symbol of peace. Olive trees have been cultivated in the Mediterranean region for thousands of years and today Spain is the biggest producer in the world with around 370 million olive trees.

Olives are rich in vitamin E and are a source of iron and fibre. They are an excellent source of antioxidants, which help to prevent damage to body cells and contain phenols that are thought to help combat cancer and heart disease.

Onions

The ancient Egyptians worshipped the onion, believing that its spherical shape and concentric rings symbolized eternity. The distinctive, pungent flavour of onions comes from sulphurous, volatile oils contained in the vegetable. These substances are also responsible for the tears during the preparation. Onions contain antioxidant phytochemicals. They also contain some vitamin C and fibre.

Oranges

The words to 'Oranges and Lemons' have been much loved by generations of children. The lyrics emulate the sound of the ringing of specific London church bells. The last three lines were added when the public gallows were moved to Newgate and the great bells of Bow were used to time the beheadings.

Oranges are high in vitamin C. They contain a variety of phytochemicals which further enhance their antioxidant qualities. Oranges also provide some folate and dietary fibre.

There are three main varieties of oranges:

- Sweet oranges such as navel, Valencia and blood oranges are for eating and juicing.
- Bitter oranges such as Seville and bergamot need to be cooked and are used for a variety of cooked recipes such as marmalade.
- Loose-skinned oranges which include mandarins, clementines and satsumas.

Parsnips

Parsnips have been cultivated for centuries and were held in high esteem by the Romans. They were used to sweeten dishes before sugar was widely available. They are a starchy root vegetable and their popularity declined following the introduction of the potato. Parsnips are a good source of fibre, vitamin C, folate and potassium as well as calcium, magnesium and phosphorus.

Papaya / Paw Paw

The papaya is an exotic tropical fruit native to Central America though the large trees are now found growing throughout tropical regions. It was allegedly called 'fruit of the angels' by Christopher Columbus and is today popular in many countries.

Papaya is rich in vitamin C and carotene producing vitamin A, as well as phytochemicals and fibre.

Peaches / Nectarines

In China, thought to be the homeland of the peach, they are a symbol of longevity and good luck. The expression, 'you're a peach' originated from the tradition of giving a peach to the friend you liked. Nectarines are peaches without the fuzz! Peaches provide vitamin C and the coloured flesh provides carotene which is converted to vitamin A. They contain other phytochemicals and fibre.

Pears

Pears have been cultivated for over 3,000 years. The Domesday Book of 1086 refers to pear trees as boundary markers in England. In 1640 there were sixty-four varieties of pear in Britain. Today three varieties account for 94% of the eating pear orchards.

Pears provide vitamin C and fibre.

- The Comice, called the Queen of Pears by the French, is considered the best eating variety and has a soft, buttery texture and sweet fruity fragrance.
- The Conference pear is long and thin with russet skin. It has sweet juicy flesh.
- The Concorde pear is a Conference / Comice hybrid. It is thought to be especially good with chocolate!

Peas

Peas are allegedly the most popular green vegetable in Britain. There are different types of peas - garden pea, marrowfat pea, mangetout and petit pois (miniature garden pea). Dried peas were a staple food of European peasants during the Middle Ages because they were cheap, plentiful and made an inexpensive, filling, wholesome meal. The French king, Louis XIV, popularized fresh peas in the 17th century. In the 19th century the monk and botanist, Gregor Mendel, used peas in his ground-breaking plant-breeding experiments studying genetics.

Peas are good for children because they are a good source of protein and fibre and are bursting with many vitamins such as vitamins A, B, C and K. They are also a good source of folate and many minerals such as potassium, calcium, phosphorus, magnesium and iron.

Peppers (Capsicums)

The pepper originated in Mexico and the neighbouring areas of Central America.

Peppers are good for children because they are high in vitamin C and provide vitamin A as well as minerals. They have everything going for them - they are colourful and sweet, and can be eaten raw or cooked.

Pineapple

The name pineapple was thought to come from European explorers who thought that the fruit looked

like a pine cone with the flesh of an apple. Originally the fruit was called anana, a Carribean word meaning 'excellent fruit'. In the 1850s, costermongers (greengrocers) sold pineapple by the piece - "a taste of paradise for just a penny a slice". Pineapples provide vitamin C, fibre and manganese, which is a trace mineral important in helping enzymes in the body to work properly.

Plums

Plums have been a part of Britain's heritage for thousands of years with the earliest recorded cultivation of the fruit during the Roman age. The British climate is one of the best in the world for growing plums. The mild and moist seasons make British plums tender and packed with flavour. Plums provide vitamin A and fibre. They contain some vitamin C and antioxidants known as phenols.

Pulses

A pulse is an edible seed that grows in a pod. Foods such as haricot beans, lentils, kidney beans, chick peas and butter beans are pulses. Pulses count as vegetables in the five-a-day scheme but only one portion, however much you eat!

Pulses are extremely good for children because they are a great source of protein, fibre, folate and minerals such as iron, calcium, potassium, magnesium and phosphorus as well as trace minerals. Some pulses also provide a variety of vitamins. As an added bonus they are often popular - particularly baked beans on toast.

Raspberries

Raspberries are thought to originate from Asia but grew so well in Scotland that, in the 1950s, raspberries were taken on a train, known as the Raspberry Special, from Scotland to Covent Garden in London.

Raspberries are rich in vitamin C and also provide folate. They contain other potent antioxidant phytochemicals and fibre.

Rhubarb

Rhubarb is commonly mistaken for a fruit but is actually a close relative of garden sorrel and is a member of the vegetable family. It was initially cultivated for its medicinal qualities and it was not until the 18th century that rhubarb was grown for culinary purposes in Britain and America.

Rhubarb contains some vitamin C and fibre. It provides minerals such as potassium and calcium.

Squashes

The term 'squash' refers to edible gourds, including courgettes, marrow, pumpkins, butternut squash, acorn squash and all the other kinds now making their appearance in supermarkets in the autumn. The squashes are native to America, North and South. Though explorers brought seeds back to Europe in the 16th and 17th centuries, squash didn't stir up any interest until the 19th century. One Frenchman, after tasting 'the new vegetable' for the first time, negatively referred to squash as "Naples' and Spain's revenge."

Squashes have the advantage of being colourful, a touch exotic. They often combine well with appealing, sweet ingredients. Squashes have a high water content, some fibre and vitamin C and the coloured flesh contains carotenoids, which are converted to vitamin A.

Strawberries

Like raspberries, strawberries are members of the rose family. They are unusual among fruits as they have their seeds on the outside. They were cultivated by the Romans who believed they could cure a number of illnesses.

Strawberries are rich in vitamin C and provide some folate. They contain potent antioxidants like other berries.

Sweet Potatoes

Sweet potatoes are a native American plant that was the main source of nourishment for early homesteaders and for soldiers during the War of Independence. They are rich in vitamin A and also provide vitamin C. They contain minerals such as potassium, manganese and magnesium as well as fibre. One colonial physician called them the "vegetable indispensable".

Sweet potatoes are often confused with yams but yams are large, starchy roots grown in Africa and Asia which don't count in the five-a-day quota. Nor are sweet potatoes related to ordinary potatoes, except that both are tubers (i.e. root vegetables).

Tomatoes

Tomatoes are strictly speaking fruit, but we tend to think of them as vegetables. Tomatoes contain lycopene which is a potent antioxidant. They provide vitamins A, C and E and also minerals such as potassium. Today China is the largest tomato producer in the world.

Serving and Cooking Suggestions

Always rinse fruit and veg before eating.

Apples

- Cut the apple into bite-sized chunks, removing the core. Leave these on a plate on the kitchen table, maybe interspersed with a few chunks of cheese.
- Try dried apple rings with a pot of natural yogurt and honey to dip them in - the fruit is nice and chewy and the honey-flavoured yoghurt hard to resist.
- Cut fresh apple into rings and serve it with a ramekin of maple syrup for dipping.
- If you have windfalls, make them into apple purée and freeze for year-round use, served with roast pork for Sunday lunch or with yoghurt, ice cream etc..
- Tried stewed apple with pear alternating with layers of natural yogurt.

Apricots

Don't forget to remove the stone where necessary.

- Try threading apricots (whole or halved) on skewers. Brush them with a little honey, and grill until semi-soft.
- Purée apricots for sauces. The sauces are especially good on pancakes, desserts, or meat dishes, particularly lamb.
- Add apricots to fruit smoothies.
- Pack them in lunchboxes.
- Dried apricots make a great snack after school and are full of iron.
- Poach in water with a tablespoon of honey and a vanilla pod for ten minutes.

Asparagus

- Always chop off the woody base of asparagus.
- Baked - place in a heatproof dish with knobs of butter. Bake in pre-heated, medium oven for approx 20 mins. You can also add some lemon juice for a change.
- Chargrilled - toss the spears in a little olive oil and place in a ridged grill pan over a high heat. Grill the spears for 3-6 minutes turning once or twice.
- Sautéed - heat a non-stick frying pan over a gentle heat and add a knob of butter. When it starts to foam, add the asparagus and toss it in the butter for 3-6 minutes. Serve with melted butter.
- Steamed - place in a steamer and cook until tender - approx. 5-7 minutes.
- Add asparagus to family dishes such as macaroni cheese, or cold to salads.

Avocados

- Slice it up in salads.
- Make some guacamole and use as a dip with raw vegetable pieces.

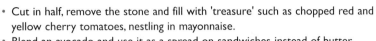

- Cut in half, remove the stone and fill with 'treasure' such as chopped red and yellow cherry tomatoes, nestling in mayonnaise.
- Blend an avocado and use it as a spread on sandwiches instead of butter.

Bananas

- Fry them (one banana per person, peeled and cut in half across) in butter until golden brown. Serve with a sprinkling of demerera or soft brown sugar and ice cream or cream.
- Bake them in their skins for 15 mins in a medium oven. Peel them when slightly cooled and serve with demerera or soft brown sugar.
- Add them, sliced, to hot or cold custard.
- For a quick banana fool, mash some banana and combine it with whipped cream or Greek yoghurt and sugar.
- Make a banana split - halve the banana lengthways and sandwich the two halves against some vanilla ice cream. Serve with chocolate sauce and hundreds and thousands.
- Use ripe or slightly over-ripe bananas in smoothies.

Beetroot

- Buy fresh beetroot, as the pickled version robs the beetroot of its natural sweetness.
- Add beetroot to salads. You can mix cubes of beetroot with segments of orange or clementine. How about a dazzling salad of beetroot and blood oranges?
- Blend with soups or search the web for a recipe for Borscht, which is a Russian beetroot soup.
- Serve cubes of beetroot, or whole baby beetroots, in a cream sauce (delicious if the sauce is flavoured lightly with cheese).

Berries

- Why not grow your own, or spend a day picking berries (away from roadsides, due to pollution)?
- Berries can be frozen. Lay in a single layer on a tray in the freezer. Once frozen they can be stored in bags.
- Use berries to decorate puddings and cakes.
- Many berries can be made into delicious jams and conserves.
- They add colour to smoothies.

Broccoli / Cauliflower

- These can be boiled, steamed or microwaved until soft but not mushy.
- Alternatively, the florets can be served raw or used in stir-fries.
- Cooked or raw it can be dipped in cheese fondues.
- Left-overs can be incorporated into a salad - for instance, mixed with left-over pasta shapes and served with a salad dressing.
- Combine broccoli and cauliflower cheese as a green and white gratin.

Butternut squash

- Bake the butternut squash whole until soft (medium oven, approx. 45 minutes), then halve, scoop out seeds and place large knobs of butter in the cavities.
- Butternut squash is easier to peel and cut once it is cooked - even pricking the skin and putting it whole in the oven or microwave for a few minutes, softens it enough to make it easier to work with.
- A quick gratin can be made by softening thinly sliced butternut squash in a pan with a knob of butter and then finishing it under the grill with the addition of a small amount of cream and some grated cheese.
- Blend roasted squash in with soups.
- Try butternut squash risotto. Bake the butternut squash whole. Make up the risotto rice as per the packet instructions. Then peel, de-seed and mash the butternut squash and mix it in with the rice. Add plenty of grated parmesan or cheddar cheese and, if liked, some thyme.

Cabbage / Spring greens

- Experiment with different types of cabbage.
- Many children prefer cabbage raw; it has a pleasing crunch.
- Red cabbage cooked with apple and brown sugar is often popular.
- One parent found that her children refused most greens but adored Chinese greens such as Choi Sum.
- Make bubble and squeak.
- Many children will eat coleslaw without questioning the cabbage in it.
- Combine steamed, chopped spring greens with fried leeks and bacon.

Carrots

- Try growing your own carrots.
- Raw carrots work well as carrot batons or in a carrot salad - finely grated raw carrot with mayonnaise and raisins.
- Carrots can be boiled, steamed, microwaved or roasted.
- Roasted carrots go well with a roast joint and can be simply roasted whole with the joint.
- Mash equal quantities of carrots and swede. Add butter and a little black pepper.
- Make soups! See page 25.
- If you make Yorkshire puddings, put small carrot batons in to the bottom of the tin and bake in a hot oven for ten minutes before you pour the batter in.

Cauliflower - see Broccoli

Celery

- Dip sticks in a little salt or a dip.
- Fill the groove with cream cheese, peanut butter, hummus or pate.
- Chop and serve in salads.
- Add to soups and then purée.

Corn on the cob / Sweetcorn

- Eat fresh (boiled, steamed, microwaved, barbecued or baked in the oven in its leaves) and dripping with butter directly off the cob.
- Tinned sweetcorn can be incorporated into hot and cold dishes or served in little piles 'neat' to complement the colours and flavours of broccoli, peas, cherry tomatoes or carrots.
- See our corn pancake recipe, page 23.
- Miniature corn on the cob is often an ingredient in stir-fry recipes and is good for dipping too.
- When you serve rice try mixing in sweetcorn and /or peas.

Cucumber

- Cucumber works well in lunchboxes and is a great finger-food for smaller children.
- Add to salads - for instance, mixed in a little bowl with peas and small apple chunks.
- Try a mix of cucumber, tomatoes, pitted olives and feta cheese.
- Don't forget crunchy cucumber sandwiches!
- Cut a cucumber lengthways, scoop out the seeds and fill it with cheese etc.

Grapes

- Children hardly need any persuasion to eat grapes as long as you buy the seedless variety.
- Bags or clusters of grapes are ideal in lunchboxes.
- Grapes can be used as decoration for other desserts.
- A mix of red and white grapes in a bowl look attractive and encourage consumption! Try pre-cutting them into small bunches.
- Combine grapes with cucumber and celery or pears for a refreshing salad.

Green beans / Mangetout

- Some children prefer these raw - leave them out when preparing a meal and see if your children are tempted.
- Use in stir-fries - cook for under a minute for mangetout, a little longer for green, or French, beans.
- If serving as a side vegetable just serve one or two to a reluctant child, to start with.
- Fry mangetout in butter for a couple of minutes, or steam.

Kiwis

You can serve kiwis in different ways:

- Peel, slice and arrange in a circle of overlapping rings on an attractive plate.
- Cut in half and eat with a teaspoon like a boiled egg.
- Cube and spear with cocktail sticks.
- Fill meringue nests with sliced kiwis and top with natural yogurt and honey or a little cream.
- Blend one kiwi with three carrots and one cored, peeled apple for a delicious drink.

Mangetout - see Green beans

Mangoes

- To remove the stone, stand the mango on its stem end and slice vertically downwards on either side of the stone. This leaves a central slice containing the stone with little flesh lost.
- To cube the mango, cut as above, then make crosshatch lines partway through the flesh. Push upward from the skin side to form a convex curve; a mango hedgehog! Carefully cut away the flesh from the skin.
- Mangoes can be sliced, diced or puréed in a variety of dishes.
- Eat on its own with a squeeze of fresh lime juice.
- Pureed, they can be used as a topping for ice cream and yogurts or in smoothies combined with other fruit.
- Mango slices are a welcome addition to green salads, adding colour and flavour.
- Make sorbet. It's easier than you think.

Melon

- Cut the melon into wedges and serve as little boats with a cocktail umbrella, or a glacé cherry attached a cocktail stick - take care with the sharp end of the stick.
- Mix the cubed or balled flesh of three melons together with some lemon juice to make a melon salad.
- Cut one of the smaller varieties of melon in half. Scoop out the seeds and fill the pit with strawberries or other favourite fruit.
- Seedless, or de-seeded, watermelon cut into chunks makes a refreshing snack.
- Provide forks to spear it up.

Mushrooms

- Fry in butter with a squirt of lemon.
- Combine different types of mushrooms.
- Don't forget mushroom risotto, which is creamy and comforting.

Olives

- Don't let your own prejudices and misgivings deprive your children of the opportunity to give olives a try. Lots of children love them. When using olives in recipes, always make sure they have been pitted/stoned.
- Avoid olives that are spicy, stuffed with chillies, pimentos or garlic. Just go for plain black (eg.kalamata) or green olives at first. For younger children, buy pitted olives.
- One popular way to serve them is in a dish with cubes of Feta cheese. Add tomato and cucumber if desired.
- Add them to pasta sauces and put olives on the top of ready made pizzas.
- Serve them on kebab sticks with ham and cherry tomatoes.
- Offer a few as a pre-meal appetiser.

Onions

- Children are not always keen on the flavour of onions eaten on their own but are often perfectly happy to eat them if they form part of a more varied dish. If necessary, you can always sneak them into a sauce by whizzing it up in a blender.
- Chop into rings and wrap in a foil parcel with a little butter and bake in barbecue coals - delicious with hot dogs.
- Onions can be eaten pickled (children often like little white pickled onions known as silverskins), or prepared as an accompaniment to a Middle Eastern or Indian meal.
- Experiment with different types of onions such as red onions and spring onions.
- Add to dishes such as Bolognese sauce, pasta sauce, soups, casseroles.
- Make onion soup with floating 'boats' of French bread topped with cheese.

Oranges

Often whole oranges are awkward for young children - too difficult to peel and too large to eat. They can also be messy and sticky. We definitely recommend the 'sports fixtures' method - cut a whole, unpeeled orange into wedges and let them suck the fruit.

- The size of clementines, mandarins and satsumas make them popular with children. Choose seedless varieties.
- A clementine in a Christmas stocking from Father Christmas always seems so much tastier than one from the fruit bowl!

- Clementines are ideal in lunchboxes, being easy to peel and not too sticky.
- Dip whole peeled clementines into melted chocolate and allow to cool.
- Serve a mixture of blood orange and normal orange segments.

Papaya / Paw paw

- Serve the fruit cut into halves or segments, de-seeded with a good squeeze of lime juice.
- Fruits that go well with papaya include mango, passion fruit, kiwi, and most berries.

Parsnips

- Try whole roast parsnips with a yogurt or sour cream dip or as a vegetable accompaniment to a main meal.
- Our children love parsnip and potato cakes. Boil or steam potatoes and parsnips and mash them together. Form into 'cakes', coat with almond flakes and fry until golden brown. Serve with redcurrant or apple jelly.

Peaches / Nectarines

- Serve halved and stoned with the depression filled with natural or flavoured yogurt.
- Peach melba, a timeless classic, is simply sliced fresh or poached peaches served with vanilla ice cream and topped with raspberry sauce.
- Baked nectarines - halve the nectarines and remove the stones. Brush with a little butter and sprinkle with brown sugar. Grill for 10 mins.

Pears

- Fry pear slices gently in butter with caster sugar. When the juices have caramelised they are ready to serve.
- Toss them in a salad with cheese and walnuts.
- Serve sliced pears with warm rice pudding.
- Poach peeled, cored pears with a vanilla pod.

Peas

- Peas can be eaten raw, straight from the pod.
- Add peas to pasta, risotto and other rice dishes.
- They can be added to soups and puréed.

Peppers

- Use as an extra topping on pizza.
- Great served sliced with a dip.
- A good way to use up ageing peppers is a cheap and cheerful variant of Spanish omelette. Chop the peppers into small pieces and fry them with onion, and at the last minute add peas. Pour on the omelette mixture. When the bottom is firm, sprinkle on some grated cheese and grill the top of the omelette until it too is firm.
- Serve as a topping on a mixed salad. Warm or cold salads made with strips of baked, roasted or grilled peppers are also delicious in the spring and summer.

Pineapple

- To test if ripe, a leaf should pull away easily from the fruit. In the shop, where you can't really do that, smell the end.
- Cheese cubes and pineapple chunks on cocktail sticks are an old favourite.
- Freeze pineapple juice in an ice cube container to make delicious cubes to suck on summer days.
- Use pineapple as a pizza topping.
- Peel, core and cut a pineapple into thick slices. Slow roast (gas mark 3 / 170°C) for 2-3 hours in water, caster sugar and a vanilla pod, occasionally basting. Top up water as necessary. Irresistable results!

Pulses

- You can add cooked kidney beans to a pie or mincemeat sauce.
- Serve tinned pulses like kidney beans cold, with or without dressing, as a salad accompaniment.
- Some children prefer baked beans cold.
- Add pulses to soups, casseroles and sauces. There are many pulse-based casseroles.
- Whizz up some hummus as an after-school snack See page 26.

Rhubarb

- The trick with rhubarb is to add plenty of sugar, so that it is sufficiently sweet.
- Choose the thinner, paler stems which are sweeter.
- Pureed rhubarb can be used to accompany oily fish such as mackerel and salmon.
- See our basic crumble mixture on page 27 and make rhubarb crumble.

Strawberries

- After cutting the tops off the strawberries, leave them at room temperature - they have far more taste than straight out of the fridge.
- Sprinkle them with a small amount of icing sugar and toss - when you are ready to eat them they will have a glossy finish.

- Strawberries are perfect for dipping in melted chocolate and allowing to set. Try some in white chocolate and others in dark and milk chocolate.
- Sliced strawberries lightly dusted in sugar then gently fried in unsalted butter are delicious too, served with ice cream or as a filling for pancakes.
- Try making strawberry ice cream. Purée 450g strawberries and beat in 300ml of double cream until quite thick. Sweeten to taste with icing sugar, stir and freeze (if the fruit is acidic, you may need to stir the mixture as it sets, to prevent it separating).
- Purée some strawberries with caster sugar to taste and the juice of half a lemon for a scrumptious strawberry sauce - good for leftover strawberries, and it freezes well too!

Sweet Potato

- They can be microwaved, steamed, baked or boiled and then mashed, to make a comforting food in cold weather, with butter melted over them.
- They can be mashed with crème fraiche and chives.
- They make a good ingredient in root vegetable casseroles.
- Cook sweet potatoes with apples - a winning combination. Peel and thinly slice the sweet potatoes. Peel, core and thinly slice the apples. Butter a casserole dish and place in it alternate layers of potatoes and apples, starting and finishing with potatoes. After each layer, sprinkle over sugar, salt, a pinch of nutmeg, lemon juice and dot with butter. Bake at the bottom of a medium hot oven for about 40 minutes, until soft. Serve straight from the casserole, bubbling in caramelised juices.

Tomatoes

- Buy or grow little cherry tomatoes or miniature plum tomatoes which children can pop whole into their mouths. Useful for lunchboxes.
- Tinned tomatoes can make a perfectly adequate substitute in many cooked recipes.
- Add sunblush or sun-dried tomatoes to salads.
- Tomatoes go well with cheese, either mozzarella or almost any other cheese, including cheddar. Serve alternate tomato and mozzarella slices, drizzled with olive oil and a few blobs of pesto, with chunky slices of bread.
- Try sliced tomatoes on toast, muffins or crumpets dotted with olive oil and grilled for a couple of minutes.
- Sliced tomatoes at room temperature drizzled with olive oil and left on the table tend to disappear!

Stir-fry Supper

Chop up veg evenly, heat some oil and put the onions and hardest veg in first. Alternatively, use a packet of ready-prepared frozen stir-fry veg.

Keep stirring around until veg are cooked but still have crunch. Add ready-made or home-made stir-fry sauce, (there are lots of internet recipes). Delicious served with vegetable spring rolls and noodles with soy sauce.

Top Ten Recipes

Here are our top ten recipes (alright, eleven...twelve...we never said we could count and we got carried away). We hope your children enjoy them too.

Pancakes

Pancakes are a great way of getting fruit and veg down.

Basic pancake mixture

Ingredients

150g plain flour
2 large eggs
450mls milk

There are two methods for making pancakes. Either put all the ingredients in a liquidiser and blend for one minute (some people add a teaspoon of vegetable oil for extra smoothness and texture). Or make a depression in the centre of the flour and pour the beaten eggs into it. Add the milk gradually, stirring from the centre until all the flour is taken up and the mixture is completely smooth.

To jazz up plain pancake mixture for savoury dishes, you can add chopped herbs into the batter before frying. Or you can flavour the batter itself by adding puréed banana, plantain, sweetcorn (see below, sweetcorn pancakes) to the basic recipe and whizzing it all up together.

Sweetcorn Pancakes

This savoury pancake needs no filling. Add a drained tin of sweetcorn to the pancake ingredients above and whizz up in the blender. Alternatively, whizz up the batter and then add the kernels whole before frying. Serve with melted butter and a little salad.

Savoury Pancake Fillings.

You can use all sorts of veg as pancake fillings, not least left-overs - cooked broccoli, carrots, peas, mushrooms, chopped spinach. Cook or re-warm your chosen veg in a pan with some cream, cream cheese or roulade and fill pancake. Sprinkle with grated cheese.

Spinach, pine nuts and roulade filling

Saute some spinach in a pan, add pine nuts and, when they have browned, add a scoop of roulade. Mix together and fill pancake.

Creamed mushroom filling

Prepare some sliced mushrooms in a pan, then add cream or cream cheese and stir together. Roll up pancake and sprinkle with grated cheese.

Tomato and onion filling

Chop two medium onions and fry in oil until soft. Add a 250g tin of tomatoes, then simmer together until sauce has reduced down. You can throw in a handful of peas if your children like them. Place a tablespoonful on the pancake, roll up and sprinkle with grated cheese.

Some sweet filling suggestions

- Puréed or stewed apple (see also Malaysian Banana Pancakes, page 25.)
- Stewed apple and pear
- Stewed apple and blackberry
- Chopped bananas and grated chocolate
- Blueberries

Try adding fruit to the batter as soon as it is poured into the pan and cook as one. For example blueberries can be sprinkled onto the batter in the pan which can be cooked on both sides as usual.

Malaysian Banana Pancakes

This recipe has never yet failed us. Even older children who turn their noses up at bananas, love this. You can make it with other fruit too. Stewed apple chunks make a good substitute for mashed banana if you want to ring the changes.

Ingredients

Serves 4
2 large eggs
1 tablespoon sugar
125g self-raising flour
4-5 bananas, mashed
Oil or butter for frying

Beat eggs with sugar. Sift flour and fold into egg, a little at a time. Add mashed bananas and mix well. Now melt oil/butter in a frying pan and when hot, spoon in mixture with a teaspoon, to make individual pancakes. Alternatively, you can empty all the mixture into the pan and cook one large pancake for cutting up. Cook until lightly browned, then turn and cook other side. Delicious hot or cold.

Carrot and Orange Soup

Soups are a fantastic way to increase your child's veg and fruit intake. This recipe is a great favourite, with a sweet flavour.

Ingredients

Serves 6
25g butter
1tbsp olive oil
900g carrots, chopped
900g onion, chopped
1.5 litres vegetable stock
Zest and juice of 1 orange

Heat the butter and oil in a saucepan. Sauté the chopped carrots and onion for 10 mins. Add the stock and bring to the boil. Cover and simmer for 35 mins. Stir in the zest and orange juice. Season with salt and pepper if necessary. Blend in a liquidiser. Return to the saucepan and heat through. You can garnish this with chopped parsley or coriander and stir in a little crème fraiche or double cream. Delicious with croutons (see below).

Croutons

4-6 slices of bread with crusts removed
oil for frying
Optional: one clove garlic / good squirt of garlic purée

Cut the bread into small cubes and fry over a medium heat, shaking and turning, until they begin to grow crisp. Remove from pan and keep warm in low oven until ready for use. If your children like garlic, turn down heat and add garlic, or garlic purée, stirring, for a further minute or two so that the garlic flavour is absorbed into the croutons.

Hummus

If you want to save a fortune and have a couple of minutes to spare, make your own hummus. It tastes better and avoids filling your children with preservatives too!

Ingredients

Serves 4
410g tin of chick peas
juice of half a lemon
squirt of garlic purée or crushed clove
1 tbs tahina paste, approx
Garnish: olive oil, pinch of paprika / cayenne pepper

Drain the chick peas and put them in a blender. Add lemon juice, then whizz. Add garlic paste, salt and tahina to taste (you can buy tahina in most supermarkets and health food stores) then blend all the ingredients together. If the mixture is too dry, add a little olive oil. Put in a bowl or dish, drizzle over some olive oil and add a pinch of paprika or cayenne pepper. Serve with vegetable crudites, warm pitta bread or toast 'soldiers'.

Vegetable curry

Even children who complain about not liking sloppy dishes are often quite happy to eat curries. You can vary the veg in the recipe below to suit your children's tastes. Serve with rice, mango chutney, slices of banana and dessicated coconut (not forgetting the poppadoms!).

Ingredients

Serves 4-6
450g cauliflower florets
450g potatoes, peeled and cubed
250g frozen peas
50g butter or marge
25g plain flour
2 or more teaspoons mild curry powder
450ml vegetable stock

Boil the cubed potatoes for 5-6 minutes and the cauliflower florets and peas for 2 minutes. Drain. Melt the butter/marge, add curry powder (start with 2 teaspoons and adjust to your children's taste if necessary) and stir for a couple of minutes. Add in the flour and then the vegetables, turning until well coated. Now add the stock, stirring repeatedly until the sauce is smooth. When the potato and cauliflower are cooked, serve.

Crumbles

Crumbles have made a come-back in a big way, recently, and are ideal for tempting children to fruit they'll enjoy. Not only does the crumble stick to their ribs, but the fruit sticks to the crumble too.

Basic crumble recipe

Ingredients

Serves 4
100g flour
75g butter or margarine
50g sugar

Put the flour, butter and sugar in a food processor and whizz them round until they are crumbs. Alternatively, in a bowl, work them to crumbs with your fingers.

Apple, rhubarb and plum are traditional crumble fruits, though you can experiment with others.

Apple and blackberry crumble

This particular recipe spells autumn in our house. If you are out on a walk, take a plastic bag and gather blackberries.

Ingredients

Serves 4
Enough cooking or dessert apples to fill your dish
Some blackberries
Sugar
Water

For the crumble: see above.

Pre-heat the oven to Gas 5/ 375°F/ 190°C and grease your pie/crumble dish. Core the apples (it isn't essential to peel them, so long as you have washed them) and slice thinly. Place in alternate layers with blackberries and sugar. Cover with crumble. Bake until crisp on top (approx 25-30 minutes). Serve hot or warm with custard, cream or milk.

Fruit Fools

Fools are very easy, light desserts. The recipe below uses raspberries, but you can adapt it for other fruit, such as blackcurrants, gooseberries or rhubarb (these will need to be cooked first and more sugar added).

Ingredients

Serves 4
300g raspberries
50g caster sugar (or to taste)
150mls double cream
150g fromage frais

Put the raspberries in a bowl and crush with a fork until only slightly lumpy. Stir in sugar. In another bowl, beat the double cream until thickened, then fold it and the fromage frais into the raspberries. Spoon into four small dessert bowls or ramekins and chill.

Banana Smoothie

Ingredients

1 banana per person
Good dollop of Greek-style yoghurt
Apple or pineapple juice to thin
Honey, to taste

Use ripe or slightly over-ripe bananas for this. Peel the banana(s) and break into pieces. Place in a blender, add some yoghurt and thin as required with apple or pineapple juice. Sweeten to taste with honey and whizz until smooth and creamy.

Tried and Tested Tips

Shopping

- Don't be scared of buying fruit or veg you are unfamiliar with. Buy a small quantity, ask the shop staff how to prepare them (or look that up on the internet, a brilliant source of recipes) and give them a go. If they are a disaster, you can all have a laugh about them and cross them off your list!
- Invite your children to choose their favourite vegetable at the greengrocer or supermarket and serve it up as 'the choice of the day is...'.
- Many expensive restaurants are known to buy in ready-prepared vegetables, fresh or frozen. So you can too, with a clear conscience, though we recommend preparing them yourself if you can - it's cheaper and there's a better chance of buying fresh local produce.
- Make sure that drink cartons say 'fruit juice' and not 'fruit juice drink'. Fruit juice is just that. Fruit juice drink tends to mean only a small percentage of fruit juice; the rest is added sugar and other flavourings.
- It's nice for children to be able to associate certain dishes with certain times of year. Hence, even where veg or fruit are available year round, try to vary how you use them according to the season. They often taste better in season too. Consider having an organic veg box delivered - seasonal fruit and veg, and the added bonus of the surprise.

Stocking up - **Here are useful items to have at home at the ready.**

In the cupboard

Tins of pulses (baked beans, kidney beans, chickpeas for making hummus, etc)
Tins of fruit in juice (fruit cocktail, pineapple, apricots, peach slices etc)
Tins of tomatoes
Tomato purée
Cocktail sticks
Skewers
Dried fruit and mixed nuts and seeds
Maple syrup or honey (for dipping fruit pieces into)
Fondue set
Tins or jars of olives
Mayonnaise

In the fridge/freezer

Frozen peas and other frozen veg
Ready made pastry
Ice cream
Greek-style yoghurt for smoothies
Fruit juice
Selection of salad veg, including carrots, for raw consumption

In the vegetable rack

A selection of fruit and veg.

Cooking Together

Cook with your children. They'll have a vested interest in the fruits of their labour. If you don't have time, hate cooking or find it just too stressful cooking with your children, then perhaps you could try to find someone else who will.

- Get a good kitchen knife. It will save you and your children cut fingers, and time - likewise, a decent apple corer and fruit zester transform the task of preparing fruit.

- Children will eat all kinds of fruit if it is in the form of ice cream. See page 20 for our easy strawberry ice-cream recipe, ideal for children to make (experts with ice-cream makers, avert your eyes now).

- Invest in some lollipop moulds. Chop fruit and mix with some juice. Liquidise and freeze in moulds. Whizz up any left-over, sad or shrivelled fruit into a smoothie then freeze it to make ice lollies.

- An easy way to get children involved in food preparation is to allow them to make their own fruit/veg salads.

- Incorporate fruit and veg into cake-baking sessions - add blueberries to muffins, grate apple or mash banana into flapjack recipes and choose recipes that are fruit-based, such as farmhouse apple sponge or fruit flans.

- Pancakes are a great way to clock up extra fruit or veg, and to use up left-overs. See page 24.

- When our fruit bowl starts to look a bit sad, we turn the contents into smoothies. You and your children can invent your own recipes or buy one of the many excellent books on the subject. Whizz up fruit in a blender, sweetened and thickened with ice cream or yoghurt and honey. The only unbreakable rule is: smoothies need to be that - smooth!

- When making jelly, include some fresh or tinned fruit, e.g. raspberries, blackcurrants, mandarin segments and pineapple.

- Puree fruit - mango, raspberries etc - to drizzle on ice cream and other desserts. Many can be frozen, portion size, in an ice cube box, and defrosted when needed.

- Dip fruit pieces, such as strawberries, banana halves or orange segments, in melted chocolate and allow to cool.

- Fruit kebabs - take care with the skewers but children love making a pattern with alternating fruits, vegetables, cheese, ham. To make them 100% irresistible, drizzle a zig-zag of melted chocolate over them and allow it to harden, before serving.

- Work within the parameters of your children's tastes. If they are pizza addicts, help them to make their own or, at the very least, give them some vegetable toppings, such as sweetcorn, pitted olives or colourful peppers, to decorate their pizza.

- *The whole is greater than the sum of its parts*. If your child dislikes a certain kind of food, try it out as part of a mixture. One of our children hates celery on its own, but will eat it in Waldorf Salad (chopped celery, chopped apple and walnuts mixed with a dollop of mayonnaise and, if liked, some added raisins or grapes).

- Try different types of mash - a perennial favourite. For example combine mashed potato with mashed parsnips, celeriac or swede for extra goodness.

- Children will often eat a veg dish if it has a gratin (breadcrumbs and grated cheese) topping.

- Try making dishes with a surprise in them. For instance, make an apple crumble with only one raisin in it and whoever gets it is the winner.

- Soups are a good way to clock up extra veg. You can purée almost any veg and add it incognito to soup or pasta sauce.

- Grate and cook carrots with the mincemeat for Spaghetti Bolognese or Shepherd's Pie.

- Invest in a small fondue pot with accompanying forks, for sweet or savoury warm sauces to dip fruit and veg into. This makes eating fruit and veg fun, and the element of who-can-get-the-most creeps in! (Try apple and cheese fondue - heat 450mls apple juice in a pan, toss together 650g grated cheddar cheese and two tablespoons of flour, then gradually add them to the apple juice, stirring continuously until the cheese has melted. Cook until thickened, then pour into a warmed fondue pot and serve with chunks of bread or raw, chopped veg on fondue forks.)

Snacks

- Dedicate a jar to a mix of unsalted nuts and raisins or a selection of dried fruit or plantain chips. They take no longer to open than a bag of crisps. If you make the mix yourself, you will save a fortune. Get your kids to choose what goes in it.

- Have a fruit bowl and buy seasonally - e.g. a bowl of cherries in summer, clementines in winter. Don't always have it in the same place, or it becomes part of the furniture! Shine apples up when you have rinsed them, to increase their appeal (especially red ones).

- As a change from a fruit bowl, try a 'crunchy bowl' filled with crunchy raw veg and salad your children can nibble from before, during or after a meal if they haven't eaten much. When preparing veg such as cauliflower and broccoli give your kids the raw stalk to eat - ours love this and it keeps them going until the meal is ready.

- Many children are very hungry when they arrive home from school. It's a good moment to serve up something wholesome, so that they start expecting variety and don't just tank up on stodge. Have a snack ready prepared in the fridge if you are working.

- See also our companion book, *'Lunchbox Pro'*, for snack ideas.

Family Meals

- Make sure there is a table you can all sit round for a family meal.

- If you are all eating together, don't serve up different meals for grown-ups and children. Just serve different size portions and be prepared for the possibility that not everyone will eat everything.

- Let your children see you enjoying fruit and veg - they are far more likely to do so themselves if it is part and parcel of family life.

- Even if you can't eat together as a family as often as you would like, try to sit with your children when they have meals, so that you can chat about your day and hear about theirs.

- Always serve small helpings. Better for your children to come back for more than to feel overloaded by your expectations.

- If your children are reluctant to try a new veg, give them just one (pea/piece of carrot/ broccoli floret) then two - one for each hand - then work up until they accept one for each finger, etc.

- Experiment with putting veg on their plates in advance - fruit and veg are colourful and can be arranged attractively - or let your kids help themselves sometimes.

- If you eat out, or go on holiday, visit restaurants serving food that is different to what you eat at home. Your children will learn about foods from other cultures and you may discover dishes and flavours they love.

- How about fruit for breakfast in the summer? Chopped fruit, e.g. dried apricots or fresh banana with yogurt on top of cereal is often seen as a treat. Some manufacturers put dried fruit in their cereal, too.

- Don't force your children to eat up all their food and don't push them if they are reluctant to try things. Just tell them that's all that is on offer until the next meal, apart from helping themselves to some fruit. They won't starve. Watching others around them trying new things might even make them feel they are missing out (anyone who has read Russell Hoban's 'Bread and Jam for Frances' will know exactly what we mean!).

- Involve your kids - for instance, in choosing recipes to cook. They enjoy emulating the look of the meals in cookery books or on the internet.

- Be canny about your triumphs - even if a dish is a runaway success, don't serve it up all the time. Your children will get bored with it.

- In summer, start meals with a selection of crudités - raw vegetables such as strips of pepper, cherry tomatoes, carrot and cucumber sticks - and a dip, before the main meal.

- Use butter or butter-substitutes on boiled or steamed vegetables, as that will enhance the taste for children and give the vegetables a nice gloss.

- Presentation is so important - make food look appetising and children will be encouraged to try it. By the same token, offer glasses of water with slices of orange, lemon or lime (or all three!) in them, to jazz them up.

- Give children the fruit and veg they like, to start with, then try to introduce new tastes gradually, combined with the ones they already like.

- Children with lurid imaginations love blood oranges - indulge their gory fantasy! See games, page 34.

- Children, particularly younger ones, can be incredibly conformist. So if your child has a friend over, find out which veg they like and serve those. Not only is this an act of courtesy, but your child is likely to join in with whatever his/her friend enjoys eating.

- If your children are trying to look cool, don't embarrass them by serving up mung beans when they have friends over - unless, of course, their friends are passionate about mung beans....

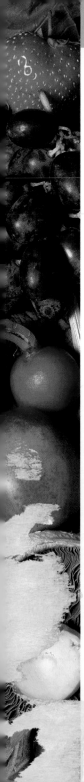

Games that make fruit and veg fun

Either when you are eating as a family or when your kids have friends over and you war to give them a teatime to remember, here are some games that make fruit and veg fun.

There is one ingredient that acts as a powerful incentive for children who are in two minds about eating fruit and veg. It is their imagination.

By harnessing your children's imagination, their love of stories and make-believe, you can make mealtimes fun and memorable.

Even older children can turn mealtimes into a sophisticated game. Ours were learning about children evacuees in World War II and before we knew it, it was gruel and blackberries for supper.

* Give appealing names to food for younger children - e.g. Peter Rabbit carrots, Flopsy Bunny lettuce (you can invite your kids to be rabbits, so long as you accept that fingers - or paws - came before cutlery).

* If your child has a particular interest - for instance, the Romans or dinosaurs or Barbie dolls, make a Roman Banquet (Italian food) or a Dinosaur's Dinner (do your homework on which dinosaurs were carnivores and which were herbivore and make up a meal accordingly) or a Barbie-Q.

* If there's a type of food in stories they are reading, offer to cook it. If the story food is made-up, work out an imaginary recipe between you, then concoct it.

* Create a fruit and veg cookbook as a holiday project - all of you could contribute

* Encourage your children to take the 'five-a-day' slogan as a personal challenge. They will start getting into the idea of healthy eating for its own sake if they als associate it with a sense of achievement. Don't worry if they don't hit the targe every time!

* To ensure variety, encourage your child to eat a rainbow of fruit and veg, i.e. five different coloured fruit and veg each day. Let them choose which. Or let them make a 'rainbow plate', finding fruit and veg for the colours of the rainbow and laying them out as such on the plate.

* Try naming vegetables, as in the wonderful children's story where peas became greendrops from Greenland and carrots, orange twiglets from Jupiter, which somehow made all the difference....

* Grow veg, and offer your children their own patch, whether in a garden or a po on the window sill. See if you can grow a fruit tree out of a pip from fruit they have eaten.

Smiley Faces - for younger children

Make teatime fun when there is a friend visiting. Ask children to make smiley faces out of fruit and vegetables, which you have cut up as necessary.

Edible Pictures

This is a more elaborate version of Smiley Faces.

Place a selection of fruit, veg and accompanying foods on small plates and in ramekins/small bowls on the table. Try to use different shapes and colours, e.g. a selection from carrot batons, cucumber batons or rings, raisins, tinned sweetcorn, blueberries, satsuma segments, peas, green beans, kidney beans, beetroot, chopped banana, pineapple chunks or rings, etc.

Give each child an empty plate and ask them to make a picture out of the ingredients. Either they have to choose a picture (and the rest of you have to guess what it is) or you tell them what you want, e.g. a person you all know (a teacher? Aunt Mildred?), a flower, an item of clothing, their initials, a sunny view, a teddy bear.

Then they must eat their picture before doing another one....

What if your favourite sport were a pudding?

Ask your kids to describe what sort of pudding their favourite sport would be, then make it! Adapt this to suit your children's interests and activities - a TV programme, a favourite book, a flower - amuse yourselves (what if Postman Pat were a pudding, or the Mona Lisa or the Prime Minister!?). Then you can all guess each others' puddings. Hmm. That banana with a lettuce-leaf in its 'mouth' has to be 'The Very Hungry Caterpillar'.

Bobbing apples

Fill a bucket or large bowl with cold water. Choose small apples to drop into the water. The aim of the game is for each child to retrieve an apple using only their teeth. They therefore need to submerge their face in the water and trap an apple at the bottom of the bucket. If the stalks are left on, however, they can 'cheat' by grasping the stalk with their teeth instead.

Afterword

We hope that this book has given you some ideas and information to tuck behind your ear, and some fruit and veg recipes that prove to be winners with your family. We have learned a lot from botched attempts at upping our children's fruit and veg intake. We have also basked in warm moments of unashamedly smug success. We wish you and your kids much fun and good luck.

Useful websites:

www.5aday.nhs.uk
www.fruitveg.com/uk
www.healthyliving.gov.uk

How many fruit and veg can you identify in this picture?